Other Books by Bonnie Louise Kuchler

Just Moms

Just Dads

Just Sweethearts

Just Kids

That's Life

Just Friends

One Heart: Wisdom from the World's Scriptures

Just Grandparents

Just Feline Friends

Flowers
for Mom

WITH LOVE

BONNIE LOUISE KUCHLER

**Andrews McMeel
Publishing**

Kansas City

05 06 07 08 09 DBS 10 9 8 7 6 5 4 3 2 1

ISBN: 0-7407-5140-9

Library of Congress Control Number: 2004114429

Book design by Lisa Martin

ATTENTION: SCHOOLS AND BUSINESSES

For Mom,
on your eighty-third birthday.
I love you.

Acknowledgments

Thanks to the "moms" in my life—
Mom, Vada, Tutu, Mimi, Nancy—
who inspired me, scolded me,
laughed with me, cried for me,
pushed me forward, held me back,
sacrificed for me, said "no" to me,
guided me, followed me,
loved me, and let me go.

Thanks to my kids—
Jill and Nate—
who awakened in me an enormous respect for my "moms."

Thanks to my agent and hero, Tom Grady.

And thanks to Christine Schillig and the gang at Andrews McMeel,
who took a risk on this book
for the sake of all our moms.

Mom, have I told you lately that I look up to you?

You challenge me to be myself—
my best self—
no matter where I am or who I'm with.

You're a terrific role model . . .

because you lead by example.

People you don't even know want to be like you.

Your gentleness brings out
the soft side of most everyone,

but you're not afraid to stick your neck out
and say what needs saying.

Thanks for keeping a sharp eye on me.

You're no stranger to sleepless nights.

Mom, have I said "thank you" lately?

Whoever said that beauty fades
should take a look into your heart.

Sure, you look great in the newest fashions,

and the latest hairstyles.

Sometimes you create your own distinctive style.

You even look great on bad-hair days,

and when you don't shave your legs.

But that's the outside,
and you really shine where it counts—
your heart.

You've touched so many lives.

I'm not just talking about the way
you reach out and make people smile
when all is right with your world.

You go beyond that.
Even when your reservoir is dry,
you give.

And give . . .

And give . . .

And give.

And you don't just give back,
you give in the first place.

Sometimes it must feel
as though we walk all over you
and take you for granted.

Sometimes you must feel alone,
even with people all around.

Mom, have I told you lately
how much I appreciate you?

You deserve more time for yourself,

more time to hang out with friends,

and more money for exotic splurges.

I wish I could make life easier for you.
If I could protect you
from life's harsh storms, I would.

But we all have to face a few dark days.

We all feel inadequate at times,

but you're a survivor.
No matter how bad the storm,
you somehow push through it
and find the sunshine.

With your special magic,
you chase away the shadows.

Did you know that any place you are
feels warm and inviting?

You could make the simplest house feel like home.

Mom, have I told you lately
how amazing I think you are?

You're a day brightener,

and a comforter . . .

a peacemaker,

and a motivator.

Through all the trials of motherhood,
you've kept your sense of humor.

Well, most of the time.

No one would ever guess by looking at you
how strong you are.

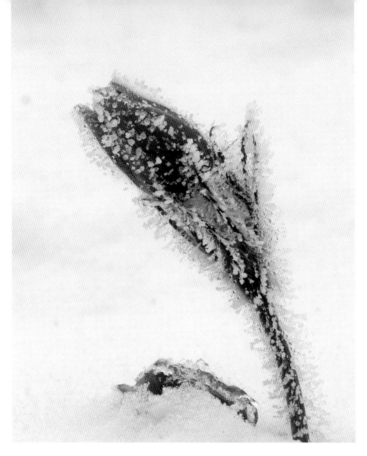

When you want something badly enough,
you are unstoppable.
Fortunately for us,
you want a more beautiful world.

You've definitely succeeded.

Imagine if everyone in the world were like you.

But they're not.
You're in a class of your own.

Even in the company of giants,
you stand out.

Yet in your genuine and humble way,
you help me see little things
and feel grateful for them.

I may never fully understand you,
with all your layers and complexities,
but I do understand how lucky I am
to be part of your life . . .

to be part of your world.

I would really miss you if you weren't around.

I would miss your hard-earned wisdom.

You know things from experience—
like when to hang on . . .

and when to let go.

I would miss your calm reassurance
in the middle of confusion and crisis.

But most of all I would miss
your unconditional love.

Mom, have I told you lately
how much I love you?

Photographer Credits

Warm and humble thanks to the "coauthors" of this book.
Your images bring depth and feeling to my simple words.

Preface: © Rex Butcher/Positive Images

Page 1: © Steve Bloom/stevebloom.com

Page 2: © Joanne Williams Photography Inc./
www.natureandwildlife.com

Page 3: © Allen R. Kuhlow

Page 4: © Leslie M. Newman

Page 5: © www.ronkimballstock.com

Page 6: © Steve Solum/Bruce Coleman Inc.

Page 7: © Ken Laffal

Page 8: © Gary Moon

Page 9: © Ron Bohr

Page 10: © Jim Steinberg

Page 11: © Richard Strange Photo

Page 12: © Michael and Patricia Fogden

Page 13: © Leslee Ellenson

Page 14: © Jose Schell/naturepl.com

Page 15: © Larry Michael/naturepl.com